Winner of the L. E. Phillabaum Poetry Award for 2020

BARATARIA POETRY

AVA LEAVELL HAYMON, *Series Editor*

MARTHA SERPAS

DOUBLE
EFFECT

POEMS

LOUISIANA STATE UNIVERSITY PRESS
BATON ROUGE

Published by Louisiana State University Press
www.lsupress.org

LSU Press Paperback Original

DESIGNER: Mandy McDonald Scallan
TYPEFACE: Whitman

Cover image: *Mythic Eruption #2*, 2008, by Gregory Botts

Library of Congress Cataloging-in-Publication Data

Names: Serpas, Martha, author.
Title: Double effect : poems / Martha Serpas.
Description: Baton Rouge : Louisiana State University Press, [2020] |
    Series: Barataria poetry | "LSU Press Paperback Original"—Title page
    verso.
Identifiers: LCCN 2019055008 (print) | LCCN 2019055009 (ebook) | ISBN
    978-0-8071-7275-9 (paperback) | ISBN 978-0-8071-7402-9 (pdf) | ISBN
    978-0-8071-7403-6 (epub)
Subjects: LCGFT: Poetry.
Classification: LCC PS3619.E77 D68 2020 (print) | LCC PS3619.E77 (ebook)
    | DDC 811/.6—dc23
LC record available at https://lccn.loc.gov/2019055008
LC ebook record available at https://lccn.loc.gov/2019055009

for my mother,
Nita Cangemi Serpas

and for the second mothers

the black-haired Mrs. Adams, Miss Lucy,
Aunt Jo, Linda, Janet, Rochelle,
Sandra, Margaret, Pam, and Pat

Nothing hinders one act from having two effects, only one of which is intended, while the other is beside the intention. Now moral acts take their species according to what is intended, and not according to what is beside the intention, since this is accidental. . . . And yet, though proceeding from a good intention, an act may be rendered unlawful, if it be out of proportion to the end.

   —after Thomas Aquinas's *Summa Theologica* (II–II, Q. 64, Art. 7)

There are four formulations to the theory of double effect: 1) The act itself must be morally good or at least indifferent; 2) The bad effect must be indirectly voluntary, not willed; 3) A good end does not justify a bad means; 4) The good must compensate for the bad effect.

CONTENTS

COMPENSATION

ACKNOWLEDGMENTS

Much gratitude to Ava Leavell Haymon for her insight and finesse; to the chaplains at Tampa General Hospital for extraordinary accompaniment; to every Cajun I've ever spoken with, especially Rochelle St. Marie, Jody Guillot, Doug Cheramie, Annette Cheramie Weaver, Lee Callais, and Cyd Duet Toups for expert language consultation; to the many friends who read these poems; to my teachers whom I sometimes call students; to my family, especially my sister Ann Serpas Hatchitt for her strength; and to my wife Audrey Colombe for top-shelf editing and literary advice, endurance, courage, and love.

Thank you to the editors of the following publications in which these poems first appeared:

Bellevue Literary Review: "Irrigation"; *Explorations:* "There Is No One Thing She Desired"; *Fogged Clarity:* "My Lot" and "On the Green Banana Leaf"; *Poetry:* "Apostrophe"; *Plume:* "Double Effect: December 31," "Pélican dans sa Piété," "Mosquito Truck," "The Comatose Have No Thermostat," "In Praise of the Unremembered," and "Née – Décédé"; *Southern Review:* "Just Call Me Beb" and "The Deuce Makes Itself."

DOUBLE EFFECT

Author's Twelve-Word Bio

Bayou: waterway
cut off from its original source
and fed by runoff

Preface

This is the island primeval. Exhaust that hangs from Latelco lines,
    pearly dust crowding those John Deere Gators that

Lift the shoulders of Highway 1, hemming in traffic and
    spraying drowsy palmettos with Little Miller

Foam across the vinyl seat, the dash, and the driver's lap:
    Beb, we almost to the ice plant. We go'n make the

Kick-off in plenty time," he says, knocking down a mulberry
    tree and splashing his riders with boue pourri.

This is the island primeval. But where are the stray
    dogs, the chestnut mare, and the rope swings,

Deckhands who passed her the hand and passed on her heart
    cut longways like a widemouth bass?

Rotting crab floats and yellow drift lines. Nothing sinks,
    except the tar balls, nothing disappears,

Everything dismantled piles up in a tide and with
    platforms endure. Hope this wind twirls this

Rain, this dishwater sky, these bald tire fenders
    slapping the bow and bumping off piers of breathless

Barnacles. Grand oaks huddle, like low-lying snow, in a
    voiceless quadrant knocked flat, except

For the sonorous inlet, the good-enough dunes. *This is*
    home to the happy, che'. Anyone wanting to die must go elsewhere.

after the Preface to Longfellow's Evangeline

Contrition

Bless me, Bayou Lafourche, for I have sinned.
It's been a thousand years since my last confession.
My sins are . . . leaving, the way the River did,

swerving for the City, pulling her braid free
of Labadieville and the Chêniére. Her dark humus.
Her rhythm. Her variation and velocity.

Engineers girdled her with levees and weirs.
Penned her in their whorehouses. Drunk on their crude concoctions.
I am heartily sorry for whatever drove her away,

for whatever drove me away, now here, cross-legged
on the batture, with you, who perhaps have suffered most,
deprived of all that suck and spoil.

What for my penance? This hopeless desire
for you, lying here with duckweed in your hair
and cypress needles across your brow?

O my heart, if I let you witness, don't tell lies about me.
O heart I've had since I was tucked, warm and willful
inside my mother, flutter as if only down lined the scale.

The Deuce Makes Itself

She looks like a brave kid waiting for the bus,
standing in the middle of the Gulf, on a shoal of plastic
yokes and jellyfish, toeing the indelible tide, in tar-gripped Keds
and a flowered suit, matching sailor hat, quilted purse,

less a stranded fish than a purposeful
island, straight bangs and hooked smile,
the sky disappearing in the shimmer
and glare of the water . . . all exuberance and grin.

She isn't in the aqualine pool with her white ski belt.
There's no radio and umbrella, no freckled lifeguard,
no copper cleavage. She bobs in the surf, the sun shines.
She feels rain that isn't falling,

surf in her head so loud it explodes language, and all
its empty promises, and the faith
she left in finger paint and exuberance
comes roaring back, exuberance   roaring   back.

\>

She loves the big-knuckled hands
that plucked her from the gray
virgules of the Gulf, the kid in Keds
drifting too close to the jetty, yanked

by one claw and dangling above
the pilings and the indifferent shore.
I am grateful, god of rescue,
but I wanted to be saved.

\>

In the end all things seek stasis
—dashing rivers drawn to branches and streams,

braided fields of wind, rain clouds
diving back into puddles and swales,

the sun rousing itself in the morning
just to lie down again at night.

Newton's five-ball cradle swings
nearly out of frame,

the third ball striking the second,
the second striking the third.

In the end all things seek stasis
—go seek all things before the end.

>

And if it rains as it often rains
on a barrier island in August

the kids play Monopoly
or The Game of Life, pink

and blue pegs in red and green
cars. The grown-ups play pedro

and drink beer. The ace is boss,
and the deuce makes itself.

Vinyl rafts simmer, crabs heat
to a seasoned pitch. The fair-skinned are

red, the brown get browner, the wax myrtle
shines through gauzy citrus scents.

\>

Imagination and memory are one,
science says. Every time

I reach back I dream a little dream
of what might have happened,

perhaps add a word from a song.
I grow more and more averse to sequence.

Instead read me a line in my own voice,
where the pitch and tone drift without fret.

\>

In pedro there's a bit
of go-fish at the end of a deal.

Ace and deuce lie
like two ends of a toy ring tower,

each worth only a point.
To bid 14–28, you need

both. Get there
or get backed.

The awkward fives score the most
but take the least.

The deuce wins what can't be lost,
gathers what's already had.

It's a life lesson: go off-card to lose
the lead. Everyone follows.

>

Optimism waits on the bayouside,
windows cranked down,

having never learned to cross the bridge
before the one she needs.

GOOD, BAD, OR INDIFFERENT

Betsy: A Mandatory Evacuation

Category Five, September 9, 1965

My father's steady behind us in his gold Dodge
My sister loose in the Dart—
No car seat or lap belt—
Watching my mother's hands
At 2 and 10, the bottom of the wheel moving
Like a pendulum across my little pit
Like a mobile, a circulation forming
That will entrance me all of my days.

Original Sleep

I was born broken
to a body put to sleep

so I dream her dreams
of escape, my wonder repelled

at no longer being confined
I must have been held

I must have been
weighed in a pan

I must have been more awake
than I've ever been

O fluorescent lights!
Wake that woman up!

Her stupor lowered
like netting

to receive a child
beating its wings

and buzzing
a female expected not to bite

Pélican dans sa Píeté

Had you never been with me,
I wouldn't hold your absence now—

Had there never been a cord,
I wouldn't have this scar, would I—

Maybe it was the whirlwind of your blood,
the amniotic undertow that had me so blazéd.

For you it must have felt
as if flesh were being plucked away . . .

A drift line, a double
heartbeat, a kerchief of hair—

In secret Betsy baptized me
into this strange sinful gulf.

I know this much:
Water is oak brown or steel gray

or so clear you see your nail beds
dipping in the fount. I've seen it rise in ditches

or lap over levees or shank down
from the sky. It hems me in

like a country club towel.
What should I have grown up on, love?

Mother Tongue

(The Playtex Poem, 1965)

I wish I could recall how much the good
    in good enough must have felt
when the black-haired Mrs. Adams
      bathed me in her mother tongue
the sound of flat *a*'s eddying
our bodies, *make do-do, make do-do*
      she must have sung
          waltzing me
in her asbestos arms
lots of waddle, lots of rouge
lots of 36-hour Cross-Your-Heart
textured polyester tapestry
pressing fleurs-de-lys
      down my cheeks.

In the end
      we will mumble our first
syllable again, if we can, as the mist grays,
an omen meant to conjure the *she*
who parted the dark for the light

for us and though I had no word
for the deep marks
down her face,
no scale for the pier
of senior themes scattered
on the chenille spread, no hands
wide enough to pluck her
from the Kleenex plunging
and rising around her head—

—I stayed stupid
when she said *I wish I were dead,* knowing

dead meant to be very still
and float away in a box
and not wake up, even
when my little cousin
stood on the kneeler to shake
her mother's shoulder and scream in her ear,
Wake up, Mama, everyone's here, and everyone was,
in the parlor or the kitchenette—

and so I was very still
and my father cooked me scrambled
eggs, and though I've longed for the dead
ever since, believing salvific
any place I am not, and though

year after year she lives and some
days bites at the hand that feeds,
that clothes, that bathes, to bite at the cord
that holds her here

where she transgresses
every social grace she once enforced
like a stay against quarantine

and though I was without consolation,
*I can't love you like I love
my own children,* the preacher's wife said,
*I feel like he did this
to one of my own children,* the teacher said,

meaning me, an almost-but-not-yet simile,

and though I moved more
than one town up, when "move
one town up" was the solution
to the utter devastation of home, so many
believing elevation brings absolution

and though somewhere some bitch
is licking a newborn, over and over
until it confuses saliva with air,
grease with fur, cleanliness
                                    with nurture

and though I've tossed small as a shell
in the tide, and even though

I will long for the francophone voice of God
and may finally feel again the unfettered press
of the black-haired Mrs. Adams, I know my voice
will call for *hers* instead, ecumenized out
of Latin, exiled from Sicilian, the silent
woman in the Polaroid passing the lather
of Ivory couth through a bleached
washcloth across the scarred stomach
of the black-haired baby
in a yellow tub on the porcelain drain,
and on that day, when I call, may she coo,
let there be sleep, in whatever language she can,
and may we both be soothed.

Patriarchy

Even as a little kid I knew
It was wrong for Mr. Gee

To have a girlfriend, especially
A cocktail waitress, and

To keep a cash box, he said, so I
Could pay for my lunch of white beans

And salt meat, and to keep beagles in a pen,
Their baby wale ears velvet as the pillows

I napped on while Miss Lucy
Swept the linoleum—*I'm going*

To see Mabel, he'd tease, and I'd
Stamp my Buster Brown feet

Indignant on Miss Lucy's behalf
And on behalf of those uncut beagles.

Double Effect: St. Joseph's Altar, March 19

Double Effect's like this:

Overall, it has to be a great good.

Imagine a St. Joseph altar:
St. Joseph and the Christ child
centered before a fan of palms.
Red-white-and-blue bunting overhead—

for some reason—

and your grandmother's Pietà
that someone held in his lap for ten hours
from Rome to JFK. Crucifixes,
a Sacred Heart, and more bread,
okra, vegetables of all kinds.

A green bowler cocked on a gold-leafed
photo of a beloved Irish priest.

His face is bigger than Joseph's.
Is *that* the double effect,
blaspheming with the clerical dead?

In the picture the prie-dieu is vacant
as a bar after closing. Is *this* the hubris,
not to give constant thanks?

Any evil here couldn't be like
taking a life to save your own
or giving that last dose of morphine
that you know will salve the pain
but shut the door.

Surely it's a great good
to remember a miracle?

You'd also have to foresee an evil . . .

what could that be?
Sufficient unto the day

that no one will eat the bread
shaped like sandals? That it
may go to waste with the poor?
Surely someone will eat
the stuffed artichokes
and all the redfish and catfish and crabs.
What could be wrong with that?

Maybe
       it's that you only have the picture,
and your people, the ones you miss like a drought,
aren't even in the frame
so when they attach it to an email
and send it to you that very day,

they mean they love you—the greatest good—
but they only break your heart.

VOLUNTARY

Changeable Letters on the Jet Drive-in Marquee

Nora drove off with a speaker
she hung from the corner of her
mirror, full-length, next to a rabbit's foot
and long Mardi Gras pearls

Its tinny voice was silent

Under a blanket on the floorboard
under some boy
under age, underweight,
under the influence

under the stars and the changeable
letters on the marquee
a tangle of footie pajamas

how safe those Buicks felt
Chryslers and Chevys
burnt butter and freshly cut grass
big heads flashing on blackout cloth

Let me tell you what nostalgia is
A glow almost too simple
the red spot at the end of the mosquito coil

a filament of smoke like a practice suture
offering to make parents of children
children of parents

separately together
in our little steel boats
our little staterooms on board one ship

all first-class
one jet lined up on the shoulder

toes sticking out
like rabbits' feet
on the floorboard

and on the corner
row where she hung up the strands
of carnival next to the little stolen speaker

Local Gods

I have always been a fan of local gods.
Whereas if the omnipresent God is ever present,
then the Cajun god is in one bar,
sitting on one stool, nursing the same
Jack and water, ready to talk—*who's ya daddy
che'*? While Cajun goddess stirs a roux,
round and round, like a wheel of fortune
spun every time to a dark-roast fan.

Whenever I get down to Golden Meadow,
I pull over at the town hall shrine
for a moment with Our Lady
of Right Here Right Now
as she opens her arms to the serpent
as it opens its mouth to cry.

Saturday Afternoon Confessional

Like the twirling figures of a cuckoo clock
(less hocus-pocus than petit chalet)

Like a speakeasy, a voice screening
        a face, an ear inclined

Near the plaster ladies' upturned hands, nothing
        up their sleeves

Like mercy padlocked
        the key in my teeth

Like a little gothic treehouse
        my soles turned out in respect

And, yes, like a disappearing box

Where on the other side
        the luminous magician's assistant
(looking so much like

My fourth-grade teacher)
        could touch my hand
and guide me into the Light

Apostrophe

See, now You are finally offstage where we can talk.

I can't see through the drapes and pulleys, it's too dark
for me to turn them into moss and oaks, too dark

for me to blink wooden risers into a bayou beautiful
in near collapse that once ran a monstrous river into the Gulf,

a scorched stew powerful only in sufficient stillness.
No monstrance, no milagro, no brown scapular scraps,

not even a woven palm frond. Just You and me.
Just me, actually, standing with hip cocked and three

fingers resting on my chin. Not even a naked
household goddess above my bed where I ache

and ache. I hate the Greeks, those bastards, for figuring
You into some kind of flesh—though that cure

is just a start. And the Romans tried, but flesh
must do more than die: it has to live. And here's what's next.

Me talking to You in Your most present absence,
without even an apophatic clue. I imagine

Your holy knees gathered to Your chin and Your arms
bound twice around your legs. I imagine Your heart

in a corner beating while You listen to my footfalls
circle from the best damn hiding place of all.

Mitzpah

Between you and Jesus, I'd choose you.
(I cannot cling to what I have not touched.)

May you look for God in me
                    and find me wanting.
May you fear me disappearing down the anchor line
just below the chop, safety stops
reversed, first, second, then third, always a lower
deep, another ledge, a wall.

Between you and God, I choose God,
       which is to choose you.
You who do not satisfy, but are closest
to the atoll or what lies beyond the atoll,
everything that conspires
                 in the dark to enchant me.

Tree Frog

I search for the little tree frog nightly
though I cannot pronounce her name
in my half-assed Cajun French

and my search is as foreign to her
as snow offshore, flecks, like
little paper bits after fireworks,

hailing the crown block and boom.
I listen for the little tree frog nightly,
I should easily find her clinging

to her bark and moss. An ol' chien
de chasse who won't come, covered in night,
resté bien, behind the fallen logs.

after Yehuda Amichai

La Porte d'en Arrière

If the front gate's too narrow,
Pass by the back.

after Matthew 7:13–14 and D. L. Menard's Cajun anthem "La Porte d'en Arrière"

Just Call Me Beb

for Joy at the Baton Rouge Best Buy

Just call me beb
Just lift more than one finger
off the steering wheel when we pass
each other in the 25, my having
assumed I could use your lane
to get around the cane truck,
and your grill smiling
like a wildcat coming on
Just call me beb, like
when you put down my catfish
poboy, having told me
it was just filleted in the back
that morning and then
putting a lagniappe of two strips
in front of my friend who ordered
the Plate Lunch instead
Beb, it's reeeally good.

Sometimes joy has to be pushed
on me, like when I tried
to cancel my order online
and then had to call the store
and I got you Joy and you
called me beb and we talked
about computers and breast cancer
and that talk you had with God
on your way home from the Lowe's
parking lot where you got your scan
Just don't let me whine, you said,
'cause nobody likes a whiner,
and if God said anything, God said,
Beb, I liked you from the first.

It was the best thing that ever happened
to me, you said.

I should call myself beb every day, and I
wonder, if I knew I was going to be reborn,
whether I wouldn't grieve extra hard
because there is Life and there is This Life,
and I would have to give up hope
for this one, the hope that some further
saving possibility could be found here, and
then wait to catch a warm front
and fly away to the next, well, then I might
be like you, Joy, listening for the rustle
of palmetto leaves in the dark
as I put my steps down on the path,
the bebettes harmonizing after the rain.

THE MEANS

The Landscape Is the Language

The swamp has a single
Discordant baseline
Insistent and full-throated
Blowing through dry palm fronds

And the long em-dash of soaring pelicans
Over elliptical knees, mossy commas
In an optional series
The chêniére's thesis
Rising above the marsh
The naked ghost trees

The saltwater interrupts
Cypress punctuates every essential
And nonessential thought

Humidity quizzes the swamp
Hangs around my ears like language lab
Headphones, till there's only
A glossary, a run-on, my mother tongue

When I speak from the heart
I step out on flotante. I shift my weight
With a pocket comb, I pull
The dead grass from the marsh
The storm decreates the water
And revises the dangling roseaus

Fallacy

We give the waves mouths
      to distinguish our joy from their anger
to pretend ecstasy won't take our lives.

I want a benevolent god to call the shots,
      to lead me to the still, yet still interesting
      waters, making me lie down under
pastures that support their own weight.

I consider being held being held
      at arm's length, the sand just left
wet by the too-close tide, the milk

moustache too close, the warm
      salty swells too close,
the flats a smooth polyester lap.

Driftwood has the sleepy imprint
      and twisted sheets of having
been deeply loved.

I sit in that forest till the pipers sprint by,
      the gull-shadows slice the beach with S-curves.
Hands shoved in jacket pockets, the wind

in my face and behind me, throwing sand,
      I want to look like I have somewhere to go,
someone waiting for me.

Diagramming the Live Oak

A couple drinks. Then what is usually
a schematic of solitude, of grandeur,

What is frequently a proof of posterity,
an assumption of unattainable wisdom—

Because we die, we all die, and the oak lives,
those imagined rings like so many glasses

Set down on a warm wooden table, same
spot, early evening after early evening—

Became, in my watery mind, a crazy diagram,
conditional, subordinate, parenthetical,

And I could not follow it for all its impossible
modifiers and negations until ultimately—

Yet not—after another drink—I ended up appositional,
swelling alongside the resurrection fern.

A Ghost Story Recanted

after the White Witch of Maurepas Swamp

Somebody gothed up your story with cautions
about a motherless girl who made off with men,
slaved in bars, then dried up to a crusty pox.

They had to redact and add revenge, cook up
that scabs-in-the-box ending. What to do
with a transgressive traiteur practicing

sacrificial sorcery in the swamp?
May I call you Kate? Forgive me,
I'm no better than a man drunk on what

has cost me nothing. Let's sit on a fallen oak.
I'll be silent while you heal wild rabbits
and tend dragonflies. How can I ask for your salve,

for the consoling voice you no longer have? Absolve me,
please, even if I shot you on the road myself.
Seraphic winged and wounded, you ignite

the swamp with mercy. And when your gender-blend
and your mulatto friend leave the hunters agape,
the white buck carries the two of you away.

Now I am repeating myself—
See I'm no better than the man who broke you
so you could bloom into Maurepas's White Wings.

My tongue split like yours, leave me dumb
at a sparkle of rain, a blue flower's phrasing:
What agony love is.

Oleander Avenue, 1927

The drowned girl is laid on a flatbed
        classmates ring her like stage lights

wide-eyed, her monolog more
        the wind driving time forward

and then like backwash they recede
        more tidal flat than transgressive dune

The truck pulls out onto
        Oleander Avenue, heads northwest

toward the parish seat
        where word has already arrived.

Parents wait in a shell lot,
        slippers and boots crunching over

hand-rolled cigarettes. The sun
        failing, one mother will

outlive a daughter, another will be spared
        losing a child half her age.

All of them will look at the girl,
        remember the one they nursed

and think now what they knew then,

        she wants too much.

Back Like It Was

There's a bit of a thermocline
>   in the Gulf's evening breeze

Afternoon and night twisting
>   where they meet

The piers come out at low tide
>   the trawlers come close

To the beach, approaching one another
>   like brothers on a field,

Like high-heeled women at a wedding
>   a careless captain bottoms

Out, filling the air with diesel plumes
>   and sending the porpoises deep

Above the trawlers' invisible trains
>   groupies vie for fish and shrimp

Each coif a delirious gull
>   holding forth from its choir stall.

>

Augusts the sisters waded into the waves
>   in their slips and broad-brimmed hats

To check the nets, to hula the silky tides
>   and expertly grab crabs from behind

Their pinchers freed from the crab net rings
        Kate settled children

On the sand, careless and whirling kites
        Rosa, a few years older, lay in the surf

Black-skirted suit with built-in cups, Jane Russell cleavage
        St. Ann a lure on her hand

She emptied the nets
        bathed in the surf on her back under a sky

That wanted nothing, her children
        her twins, her body self-possessed.

>

My mother didn't like sand
Didn't care for anything
        hitching a ride on her hips

Something else she'd have to sweep
        up and dump in the kitchen can—
The kind she commanded with a step
        and didn't need to touch—

Anything she'd have to brush or bleach or scrub

Sometimes the truth has to wear on me
        the way old jetties appear at low tide.

>

Back like it was, isn't that what I wanted,
     an off-kilter pier—pared heartwood, a bit of dock,
                old egg sinkers and leads, barbs
        snipped off their hooks, lures
                   wedged between pillar and plank
          almost like cleats, no weighted lines—leaves
     just enough jetsam to breast up to.

Generation

He doesn't remember anything.
His skin half amniotic wash,
His nombril an "O" of surprise,
The cloak of endometrium still a glow
Around his shoulders' down. And she

Doesn't remember that she doesn't remember
Anything, even that memory
Is poor substitute for the deeply
Familiar, the uncanny comfort
In recognizing one's genius.

Last night, sleepless, she prayed my fingertips
Like beads, saying the prayers, confused enough
By "among women" to offer gurgles
Each time those trochees came around.

So when I laid his head on her enormous breast
And she didn't recoil or cover her heart,
He closed his eyes and took his hand
In his mouth, as if consuming her touch.

Are You My Mother?

The butterfly throwing herself
            against the hayloft window

    is not my mother

The dog chained to a single-wide

    the owl

        that the car clipped under the full moon

    the injured cow, the caged bird

are not my mother

    Lie down. Pay two hundred bucks.
    Lather. Rinse. Repeat.

Martha, are you grieving over
    Golden Meadow leaving?

The parting you were born for:

    release the mother you mourn for.

after Gerard Manley Hopkins's "Spring and Fall"

Yachtzee

One night Mama and I have the same dream.
    First me, coming upon bodies

musing over a board game,
    smoky in half-light.

I don't know how to play,
    I say. No one

will teach me the rules.
    When I wake in Memory Care,

lying next to her, my mother,
    in the bed my parents shared,

she is speaking clearly in her sleep:
    I don't know how to play, she says.

I'll just watch y'all.
    And it breaks my heart she couldn't

follow the numbers to the music
    before she broke my father's heart.

I'm Tending a Bit toward Living These Days

I'm tending a bit toward living these days.
The functions of grief are losing their gloss

just in time for me to bury you or rather
tuck you into the marble drawer

beside your mate. Is there
a Ladies' Altar Society anymore?

Will someone cook a roast,
her husband's name in freezer

tape on the pan's glass bottom?
Remember? the chill of the mahogany parlor

the prayer cards in crystal dishes
the sprays beside the open graves

a phony spring trucked over (by magic, it seems)
in November as the Town Cars arrived?

Remember how laughter broke us
in the limo, we were pâmmed, about lipstick

or Armor All, while drivers slowed their radios
and daytime headlights flashed around us.

Just in time, you decide to stop eating meat
when all you'd eat was meat, all I eat

is meat and once only the meat you cooked,
a nonnegotiable that drove my father nuts.

Just in time they check your vitals
daily. They record your weight. They

want to keep you comfortable. I tell them
you were never comfortable, the nearness

of you made me uncomfortable like drinking
iced water too fast. Only fevers had you

sleep in my bed. *So I can feel you*, you'd said,
your distorted face a supermoon

in relief, hurtling toward me,
your skinny hand a visor on my brow.

Did you sleep? I did. The felt so hot under my chin.
You were listening for something, a clicking

a Dictaphone, you were desperate for it,
for an obligation to snap shut.

If I were a tree, you would overtake me
      like a strangler fig

like mildew if I were a plaster wall
when you die, your body will cling

to mine like a conjoined twin's.
I will tend your dying

a bit more like living now, the creeping tide
always leaving something behind.

In Praise of the Unremembered

Not forgot, as if the mind had left a book
on the table, closed the front door,

and walked downstairs to the car.

Not the talismans I still hold—a digital watch,
the stipes of a broken cross
dangling from my rearview mirror,
a blues harp's clear C, her flushed chest,
a boy ribbed white and leaning from a window
of a train station in some city
I've since forgotten—it goes on and on.

Unreliable historian, I can put these
together for the surgeon, nervous I may leave out
the one ache, the pill, the meal that will
                 save my life. It goes on.

I can arrange for him the most tedious
clichés, the drive-thru morals
of fear, perversion, shame.

Or sometimes, even exuberant
good fortune while around me
at the table the arid smokers lose.
O the annoyance of the unlucky
when I am not one of them. Leave
me alone. Must I pay what I owe
with my happiness? It goes on.

But what is unremembered,
I can't tell you a thing about.
I have no beliefs, thank God,

just a weird kind of faith, like my dog
standing at the front door, ear cocked
         toward nothing.
He feels me while I am
blocks away. I love the unremembered
like that. It's my whole life, what I cannot plot.

after Jane Kenyon

Compassion Requires
                    I Imagine I'm Something Else

The imagination stripped is beauty,
                    beauty of dazzling gratitude:
            back to us the undiscovered in us,
what we thought, but could not see, from where we stopped.

What is beautiful in me is so small
as if a barb of driftwood, carbon
            and oxygen knitted by earth and air,
    kneaded by the sea, then brought
                    back to the air by fire settled
            in my chest.

The whirl rises out of what is so small,
    so small it begins as a particle
            of hardwood and ends
                    as a flickering blue and yellow voice.

Doxology

Do you believe in Jesus? Patrick asks.

I believe in spikes that fix us to one another,
        in naked chests under cloaks

in grief wrung to anger
        betraying our barrenness

in spontaneous generation, fertility
        without seeds

in indulgence

that coming out of the cave is resolution

that someone can, must breathe for us

I believe in what each of us sings

COMPENSATION

To the Tripmaster

Pike's Market

When I cry the street looks brilliant.
Gas lamps hollow the evening's haze . . .

I am peaking and looking to dock,
but you—my ordinary, my rubric, my creed—have a quest for me

for a balcony, uphill . . . a flyer, a hoop torch,
a Ferris wheel. Its bulbs tick neon,

tock tar blots . . . spins my observations—
you—my séance, my succulence, my sage—

tattoos the night . . .
                        . . . dials me back to a hard bump
off Miss Daisy's seesaw:

I am five, at her school's-out-at-last boucherie. The teachers
            down Little Millers and peel boiled crabs . . .

I . . . in my snail-appliqued seersucker sun
dress . . . am a teacher, too. I teach fear . . . already
            what the mothers know too well . . .

. . . The asphalt rushes in, separates like gravy
in need of a dollop of Kitchen Bouquet.
The sweet clover overtakes a boat of rough cement . . .

I didn't want to jump, I tell my shrink when she asks . . .
I tell her, *I still knew, this high,* that the overripe gondolas

swaying into the black air were empty
(besides I could never survive the ride).
I looked down into the swells as if from a sloop,

where wind riffles the water like a host of breaths,
. . . all of us safe in the aft. Look—my lot, my lottery—

a bubble in the sluice teases the gutter,
such a shiny surface, what a pinball . . . flashing
between a dozen tread marks keeping us afloat!

My Lot

Across the street most mornings
the field's far patch looks shorn

The light has a brilliant edge
that evens across the grass

But it's not cut, really

This morning though the whole of it
is brown with billets and I remember
I lost you

I took the blade of my crazy
and cut us down

Now the birds come for the confused insects

They eat the field   They fly away

Née – Décédé

We were seated around the Thanksgiving table—
turkey, stuffing, potatoes au gratin—
eight or ten of us, when I noticed,
as I passed on the green beans and slivered
almonds, that they were all dead:

gelatin-eyed, orifice-oozing, putrefying dead.
I hadn't detected the strong smell above the broccoli
casserole and crusty Brown 'N Serve rolls.

I had been passing the wine, passing the water,
talking to myself about my affairs.

As their fingers lifted slightly from the table,
I laid coins on their eyes and kissed their brows.
I freed the dogs, who seemed warm, from their filthy pens.

One shouldn't look for the living among the dead.

Back at the farm where my father, dishes done,
moves a stick through ryegrass,
and a sharp-tailed snake heads for a thicket.
He wanders below Douglas firs and
smokes a Kool cigarette.

In the mornings I lie with him in the orchard and watch
the elk calves leap like static.
Sometimes a young bull. Mostly
cows clowning, distracting us while their cow
friends unlace Liberty apples
                    from the lowest branches.

He hasn't aged. His nose is still broken
and his knuckles are a size too large.
For July his skin is burned patriot red,
and his eyes are green, green, green.

The hyphen between his dates is so tiny, carved
into the mausoleum's marble, it is a freckle,
half an ellipsis.
It's meant to pull the years one
on top the other. It's meant to erase
itself, like an iris wipe before The End.

On the farm I cut the grass with a push mower.
I try to save the wren's nest I dislodged
with the cane knife—his—
that I had been swinging through the brambles.
I nail new shingles on the porch steps when it rains.

Every morning I bring you tea in bed is his tomorrow.
The tray empty, the kettle and steam quiet,
the bricks fire-polished and weightless as they fall.

The Comatose Have No Thermostat

Chris, fâched and broken-hearted, flipped his car
on a turn. Just enough water in the ditch
to drown him, but not enough to take his life.

Damn near death, he sweat through sweat,
his vent an electric chair. Mother and sister fought over
the plug, one pulling out, one pushing in.
Just enough glow on the Lite-Brite scan
to leave them the choice.

Sprung from ICU, he flailed across the bed—
straight-armed, first right then left
like a varsity cheer, his hands
never coming together in resolve or rest or prayer.

He made it to a semiprivate crib,
his fingers caught in the mesh like pinchers in a net.
His wavy hair and dry brow scoring a 98.6.

O the guilt of that woman who was ready to let him go!
After three months, he reached out for the girl
who threw him over and put a hand on her belly.
He couldn't talk, but he knew the little fish was his.

He was the father all right. Only who that father was
come out the primordial ditch none of us could say.

Irrigation

We steal water when we make rain, the way
everything I have is from somewhere else,
from someone else, this bag I am

the riverbed looks scalded
but the wound is full thickness
and elsewhere

in a variegated field or on a lawn
of grass named for a saint
or a saint once removed

we can't walk on it
eventually it comes up
dry and tired

the way we wear everything out
especially each other
listening with heavy feet

unlike the river which never tires
whose pocket we pick
down to the lint

On the Green Banana Leaf

I think, in the end, we must just fall
under the weight of
                              all our undigested measures
The brown anole
                    on the green banana leaf
tugging at its sleeve
          drawing the skin into its boat-shaped mouth
                    sipping it really
like hot coffee and then gulping a second raft of scales

I've seen its yellow diamonds shine
          for decades now but missed
how slow its first loosed steps are, how vulnerable
          it might be to a bird
                         or a human child
who could lift it easily by the tail
                                   like a kite

Mosquito Truck

Mauve night air.

Palmettos and chinaberry trees
oyster shell drives

tassels
of moss

a heavy
old all-so-familiar film

we take in from our vinyl loges.

Field crickets. Frogs. Our
forearms stretched maroon from the sun.

Under every camp a Ford
and a trailer, a porch swing
and propane burner.

The deep hiss and hum
of the mosquito truck

blowing kisses behind itself
like a festival queen in a hurry,

up and down the old part
of the Island, the fog muscling it along.

Bottles and go-cups
part the wake
and an organist cues the moon.

L'encensoir recedes, the hum fainter,
the drapes glowing,
all manner of thing well.

Flat Water

The morning's all flat water and pancakes,
a mosquitoless breeze and sunflowers in relief
before a Mediterranean-blue Gulf,
its tar balls and salty weight thinned
as if *it* were popping eggs instead
of those August crabs, fat
and fecund, chilled in the chest
next to the top of our wedding cake,
a Blackened Voodoo and church key,
spent ice bag floating in the swill
like pristine jellyfish in the shallows
that wouldn't dare sting us today.

for my wife

I No Longer Have the Moon

I no longer have the moon
I've laid it on the inky Gulf
next to my virginity
a rumpled half slip on the bedspread

a smoky wasp's nest of all the eggs I sent
on their way   (thirty-eight years of half-me's)
on my way to having you—
this absence! our new new moon

Double Effect: December 31

. . . it is natural to everything to keep itself in
"being," in as far as possible.
—AQUINAS

Goodbye Year-I-Almost-Died
        the bridge closes behind you
        in closing to you

it opens to me, a foreseeable
        but unintended consequence
        of your passing

the one-armed tender, drunk
        and mending nets
        will wave me through

Year-I-Almost-Died, I pass you
        the peace
        one day I'll forget who you are

Down the bayou
        I make the veillé
        turn down a shell road

I get down at the levee
        I like to sit on the grass
        and be with the stars

I still like to drive the colors
        wild I like to pray
        bromeliads on fire

Year-I-Almost-Died
        I curse and bless you
        for all your magic

and all your monstrosities
            the lizard that eats its own skin
            the fern flaring after rain

And nights I laid my back on the waves
            I laid my hands at my side
            the darkness erasing the tracers

I stood on silver guardrails
            I swallowed the streetlights
            the coyotes in the mist-draped field

Year-I-Almost-Died
            you were that promising date
            that began with a chilled corsage

and ended on a rainy doorstep without a kiss
            you were that toast, that pyrotechnic
            display and its acrid smell

Year-I-Almost-Died
            we slept together in a twin bed
            while the dog curled on the floor

O what a better companion he is
            he rounds my sleep
            and covers my dreams

Year-I-Almost-Died
            the bridge closes behind you
            and in closing it opens for me

There Was No One Thing in the World That She Desired

Madame Pontellier walked down to the beach,
thoughtless under a hot sun, but Edna

walked into the deep, chilly water. *All along
the white beach, up and down, there was no*

living thing in sight. Was she on my mind
when I abandoned my children

to their little follicle prams? (Beautiful birds,
they will never have broken wings.)

The doctor, or his belief in her, made her
think of turning back, but it was too late.

Her white arms reach past me
with long, sweeping strokes,

past the break line and
into the gray-green wash.

Me, I stand on the shoal
in my tar-gripped Keds

and flowered suit, matching sailor hat,
and quilted purse, where

the backwash and the waves collide
and my bobby socks stretch

into foam pearls
across the island primeval.

Coda: To Hell, Bébé

To me you no longer a part
De feeling I had for you is faded
like papa's dungaries

You put a hole in my heart like
De one in mamere's step-in

Me I got a career at Ledet's
I got no time to think of you
except when I look at the chicken
I can't help but think of your sexy
body when I see them

It's too late for "Che' bébé! I love you
and I'm sorry."
Too late for pirogue rides—too late for
kisses in de cabon
I'm haunt for de way I felt for you
You used me
You used me
You used me

You moodee bête

Cyd Duet Toups
Annette Cheramie Weaver
Becky Guidry
ages 14, circa 1980

CAJUN FRENCH–ENGLISH GLOSSARY AND NOTES

"Anyone who wants to die must go elsewhere.": from Lafcadio Hearn's
Chita: A Memory of Last Island

"Are You My Mother?": also the title of P. D. Eastman's 1960 children's classic

batture: bayou side

bebette: frog or monster

blazéd: stoned; "lit"

boucherie: a community pig butchering and roast

boue pourri: "rotten mud"

cabon: small out-building

ché (cher) \sha\: dear

chêniére: oak ridge

chien de chasse: hunting dog

comme ça: like that

fâched: angry

flotante: floating marsh vegetation

get down: get out of the car; originally to descend from a horse or boat

haunt: embarrassed

John Deere Gators: four-wheeled utility vehicles

l'encensoir: censer

lagniappe: "a bonus"; an extra spoonful

Madame Edna Pontellier: protagonist of Kate Chopin's *The Awakening*

make do-do: go to sleep

make the veillé: go visiting

mamere: grandmother

moodee (maudît) bête: damn thing

née – décédé: born – died

nombril: navel

pâmmed: breathless with laughter

pass you the peace: exchange peace greeting

pedro: a trick-taking card game; the name given the trump five and same-color five; each is worth the highest number of points

pélican dans sa píeté: "pelican in her piety"; the image of the pelican vulning herself was adopted by the Church as a Christological metaphor. One possible origin is an ancient Egyptian myth about a bird that set her nest on fire, killing her chicks, and then resurrecting them with her own blood.

prie-dieu: kneeler

resté bien: "rest well"; old French compliment for a good photographic likeness achieved by the subjects holding still; in contemporary use translated literally, "you stayed so good."

roseau cane: a marsh grass

stayed stupid: to be rendered speechless

step-ins: panties

"This is home to the happy.": from Longfellow's *Evangeline*

traiteur: faith healer

White Witch of Maurepas: New Orleans ghost tale included in Jeanne deLavigne's *Ghost Stories of Old New Orleans* under the title "The Swamp Witch"

Yachtzee: original spelling of the popular dice game Yahtzee

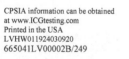

9 780807 172759